HOPE AND RECOVERY

THE WORKBOOK

CompCare®Publishers

2415 Annapolis Lane
Minneapolis, Minnesota 55441

ISBN 0-89638-198-6

Interior design by Lillian Svec
Cover design by Jeremy Gale

Inquiries, orders, and catalog requests should be addressed to
CompCare Publishers
2415 Annapolis Lane
Minneapolis, Minnesota 55441
Call toll free 800/328-3330
(Minnesota residents 612/559-4800)

5   4   3   2   1
94   93   92   91   90

*In memory of the addicts who
died before finding recovery*

Acknowledgment

*Warm gratitude to Rob—for reviewing the first draft
and for being Rob*

Contents

Introduction

The first time many of us saw the Twelve Steps, we thought they were much too simplistic to help us recover from something as destructive and complex as sex addiction. But the longer we studied the Twelve Steps, the more we understood that our first impression of them was limited, and therefore incorrect.

The Twelve Steps are, indeed, filled with healing insights and support—*if* we are willing to put time and effort into applying them to our lives. This workbook is designed to help recovering sex addicts and codependents to sex addicts personalize and apply the Twelve Steps, thereby making each of the steps useful in their daily lives—for *all* stages of recovery.

The questions in this workbook rather closely follow the text of *Hope and Recovery*. They are designed in such a way that they can be worked on alone and in private, or as an integral part of group discussion. But regardless of the circumstances in which you use this workbook, it will prove most helpful and meaningful to you if you do the following: *prior to responding to each set of questions, read the portion of text that corresponds to the questions* (page numbers referring to the *Hope and Recovery* text are in parentheses at the beginning of each section of questions.) And remember, recovery is a *process*. Resist any tendency you might have to hurry through the material. This workbook will be most valuable to you if you study the text and respond to the questions *after* taking time for some personal reflection.

The questions in this guide were developed by the coordinating author of *Hope and Recovery* as an outgrowth of sponsorship and other Twelve Step work with addicted people.

I. The Twelve Steps as a Program of Recovery

Before beginning the first section of the workbook, take a few minutes to read the introduction to the *Hope and Recovery* text entitled "The Twelve Steps as a Program of Recovery." It describes a newcomer to the Twelve Step Program—how he was compulsive about sex and was, at first, compulsive about recovery as well. Have you been impatient with yourself or compulsive in your recovery? If so, in what ways?

The authors encourage you to work the Twelve Steps in order. As you read through each of the Twelve Steps, ask yourself if you have made conscious efforts to apply them to your daily life. After some reflection, which of the Twelve Steps would you say you have made the most effective use of in your life?

After some reflection, which of the Steps would you say you have neglected to make use of in your life?

You can begin to use this workbook by reading pages 1-10 of *Hope and Recovery* and then answering the questions about Step One, starting on page 4 of this workbook.

Am I Really Out of Control?

(pages 1-10)

1. How did you respond the first time you heard the words *sex addict*?

2. Is your current response to the words *sex addict* different than your response to these words the first time you heard them? If so, how has your response changed over time?

3. What is your definition of *sex addict*?

4. Does your definition of *sex addict* help or hinder your recovery? In what ways?

5. What is your definition of *acting out*?

6. Does your definition of *acting out* help or hinder your recovery? In what ways?

7. What is your definition of *powerlessness*?

8. Does your definition of *powerlessness* help or hinder your recovery? In what ways?

9. How have you attempted to stop, limit, change, modify, or otherwise control your obsessive sexual thoughts and compulsive sexual behaviors?

10. How have you been dishonest with yourself and with others regarding your obsessive sexual thoughts and compulsive sexual behaviors?

11. What promises regarding your obsessive sexual thoughts and compulsive sexual behaviors have you made to yourself, to your Higher Power, to members of your family, and to other people?

12. How have you tried to hide your compulsive sexual behavior?

13. How have you tried to explain, justify, or rationalize your compulsive sexual behavior to yourself and/or to others?

14. Describe some things that have happened in your life as a result of your compulsive sexual behavior—circumstances that perhaps have led you to acknowledge your powerlessness:

15. What do you think your life will be like in *five years* if you do not work a program of recovery now?

16. What do you think your life will be like in *ten years* if you do not work a program of recovery now?

17. What is your definition of *unmanageability*?

18. Does your definition of *unmanageability* help or hinder your recovery? In what ways?

19. How has your compulsive sexual behavior affected the following aspects of your life:

   ● your career?

   ● your emotional development?

   ● your relationships with family and friends?

   ● your financial security?

- your spirituality?

- your physical health?

- your mental health?

- your integrity and ethics?

- your self-respect?

- your values and standards?

- your life goals and objectives?

20. Do you occasionally fall into what addiction professionals sometimes call "euphoric recall"—a tendency to lose sight of your previous powerlessness and unmanageability and an increased longing for the "good old days?" If so, describe how and when this has happened in your recovery:

21. List some ways that you make use of the First Step each day of your recovery:

22. Have you written a history of your acting-out behaviors and reviewed it with your sponsor and/or others? If you have not yet written a history of this kind, do so at this time on a separate sheet of paper. Then, based on this personal story, respond to the following questions.

23. What emotions did writing your history trigger for you?

24. What were the most difficult things to write about in your history?

25. What were the most difficult things in your history to tell another person about?

26. In the process of writing your history and sharing it, what have you learned about yourself, your addiction, your own recovery, and the recovery of other addicts?

There Is Help
(pages 13-17)

1. Are you willing to believe that your addiction can be arrested *only* if you seek help from a power other than your own will and determination?

2. How effective have will and determination been for you in dealing with your addiction? How does this relate to the First Step?

3. How have you, in the words of Alcoholics Anonymous, tried to "play God"?

4. In what ways is a group of recovering addicts more powerful than one addict alone?

5. Have you ever thought that you were somehow *born defective*? If you have had this thought, explain it in more detail here:

6. In what ways have you already been restored to sanity?

7. What is your definition of *spirituality*?

8. Does your definition of *spirituality* help or hinder your recovery? In what ways?

9. What is your definition of *religion*?

10. Do you incorporate *spirituality* and *religion* into your recovery? If so, how do you do this?

11. Do you struggle with certain blocks to your spirituality?

12. How can you make use of Step Two to overcome these spiritual blocks?

Accepting the Help
(pages 19-25)

1. Do you really *want* what the Twelve Step Program has to offer? How do your behaviors reflect your answer?

2. In what ways are you currently resistant to accepting Step Three?

3. The authors of *Hope and Recovery* tell of using Step Three to free themselves from obsessive thinking. List examples of obsessive thinking that you have struggled with in the past but are now free from:

4. Do you still struggle with obsessive sexual thoughts? If so, describe the nature of these thoughts:

5. How can you make use of the Twelve Step Program to permanently free yourself from obsessive sexual thoughts?

6. The authors write about defining a Higher Power. Who or what is there to protect you? Describe *your* Higher Power:

7. How does the Twelve Step Program fit with your spiritual/religious beliefs?

8. The authors note how easy it is to forget the amount of time they once devoted to their acting-out behaviors. Think back to an average day when you were acting out your addiction, then write a detailed description of that day here:

9. During your active addiction, how many hours each day did you spend planning your acting-out behaviors, acting out, covering up your acting-out behaviors, and feeling shameful about those behaviors?

10. What did you give up in your daily life in order to find the amount of time and energy you needed for your acting-out behaviors?

11. Now, in contrast, write a description of what you do *each day* in order to work your recovery program:

12. How much time do you spend on your recovery, particularly compared with the time you used to spend acting out?

13. What do you believe you have gained and continue to gain with your new investment of time and energy in recovery?

Threshold to Self-Knowledge
(pages 27-31)

1. The first part of this section identifies shame as a barrier to recovery. How has shame been a part of your addiction?

2. How has shame made it difficult for you to work the Fourth Step effectively?

3. The authors remind us that ''Self-honesty is fundamental to this Program; we really cannot recover without getting to know ourselves.'' In what ways have you been reluctant or unable to face yourself *as you are*?

4. How has the language you've used to describe your acting-out behaviors either minimized or magnified your behavior and its consequences?

5. What did you hope to gain or avoid facing by using less than accurate language to describe your acting-out behaviors?

6. If you have not yet completed a *written* Fourth Step—what have you said to yourself about this unfinished business?

7. What do you believe you have lost by not completing a Fourth Step?

8. What do you believe you need to do in order to begin the Fourth Step process?

9. If you have completed a Fourth Step, what do you believe you have *gained* in doing so?

10. Each time we gain in recovery, we lose something from our addiction and the addictive process. If you have completed a Fourth Step, what do you believe you have lost from your addiction as a result?

11. What was, for you, the most difficult aspect of working the Fourth Step?

12. What was, for you, the most rewarding aspect of your most recent Fourth Step?

13. How will you know when it's time to do another Fourth Step?

From Shame to Acceptance
(pages 33-36)

1. If you have not completed a Fifth Step, find someone who has done so and ask that person what he or she has gained from it. What benefits are you likely to derive as a result of completing your Fifth Step?

2. How does the Fifth Step process differ from a confession?

3. What is your definition of *forgiveness*?

4. Does your definition of *forgiveness* help or hinder you in completing a Fifth Step? In what ways?

5. If you have completed a Fifth Step, review what you have gained in doing so:

Commitment to Change

(pages 39-41)

1. In what ways are you ''entirely ready'' to have your character defects removed?

2. List some character defects that you particularly look forward to having removed:

3. How have these character defects affected your life and harmed you?

4. List some character defects that you are reluctant to have removed:

5. How have you seen the Twelve Step Program work in the lives of other people? What character defects have you seen removed in other people?

6. How has the Twelve Step Program worked in your life? What character defects have been removed or modified as a result of your use of the Steps?

Asking for Grace

(pages 43-46)

1. What is your definition of *humility*?

2. Does your definition of *humility* help or hinder your recovery? In what ways?

3. Are you seeking the wisdom of other recovering addicts? If your answer to this question is yes, how are you doing this?

4. If you are not seeking the wisdom of other recovering addicts, what do you attribute this to?

5. Do you really *listen* at Twelve Step meetings and apply the group conscience in your life? If your answer to this question is yes, how are you applying to your life *today* what you have learned?

6. If you are not listening at Twelve Step meetings and you are failing to apply the group conscience in your life, what do you attribute this to?

7. The authors of the *Hope and Recovery* text point out that one method of using the Seventh Step is to ask other recovering addicts to tell us how they see our recovery proceeding. Ask at least three people who know you and who are also working the Twelve Step Program to describe the changes they see in you. Take notes here on what they tell you -

   • Person One:

   • Person Two:

   • Person Three:

8. The authors suggest the difficulties and risks of trying to practice Step Seven while in "slippery places." Describe some situations that you have placed yourself in that make recovery more difficult for you:

9. Read "The Promises" (pages 83-84 in *Alcoholics Anonymous* or page 326 in *Hope and Recovery* text.) How are the Promises coming true for you? List some things that you thought you'd never be capable of doing but are now able to do—as a result of working the Twelve Steps:

10. The authors suggest that you make special use of the Seventh Step Prayer (page 76 in *Alcoholics Anonymous* or pages 45-46 in *Hope and Recovery* text.) Copy this prayer in your own handwriting each day for a month, then record here what you learn from the prayer each week-

- Week One:

- Week Two:

- Week Three:

- Week Four:

The End of Isolation

(pages 49-52)

1. Write the names of ten people who have been harmed by your addictive behaviors -

   ● person harmed:

   ● person harmed:

   ● person harmed:

   ● person harmed:

   ● person harmed:

   ● person harmed:

- person harmed:

- person harmed:

- person harmed:

- person harmed:

2. Return to your list of people harmed by your behaviors. Next to each name on the list, write what you did or did not do that resulted in harm to that person. Then, go over the list with your sponsor, with other group members, and/or with someone who has heard both your First and Fifth Steps. (Have you included *yourself* on your list of persons harmed? If not, reread page 50 of the *Hope and Recovery* text.)

3. After discussing with others your list of people harmed by your behaviors, take some time to pray and meditate. If it then seems appropriate to do so, make changes to your list.

4. Resentments are identified as blocks to serenity. List the people you resent and the reasons you resent them:

5. How are you hindering your recovery by holding on to resentments?

6. Write a forgiveness letter to one of the people on your resentment list. Each day, read this letter and pray for that person's well-being. Do this until the resentment you feel toward that person is gone. Then, use this same process with each of the other names on your resentment list. What do you sense you will gain from doing this?

Restoring Relationships
(pages 55-59)

1. What is your definition of *the process of making amends*?

2. Does your definition of *the process of making amends* help or hinder your recovery? In what ways?

3. Return to your list of people harmed from the previous section (page 35 in this workbook.) Next to each name listed, write what you think would be appropriate amends for the harm you have caused that person. Then, show this list to other recovering addicts who have themselves worked the Eighth Step. (Sharing with other addicts in this way will ensure that in making amends you are neither causing additional harm to yourself or others, nor avoiding something that might help you with the important process of making amends.)

4. Begin the amend-making process with a person on your list. Then, following each act of self-forgiveness, write your thoughts and feelings here:

(1)

(2)

(3)

(4)

(5)

(6)

(7)

(8)

(9)

(10)

Maintaining the Growth
(pages 61-64)

The authors identify two kinds of Tenth Step inventory—the *spot check inventory* and the *nightly inventory*. Try the following exercise in order to build the *nightly inventory* into your schedule—each night for a month, make a conscious effort to set aside time prior to getting ready for sleep to inventory the day that has just passed. In the journal provided at the back of this workbook, write down when, during that particular day, you were wrong:

(As you do this, however, pay attention to how forgiving you are of yourself. If you find that you are being perfectionistic, you may want to make additional use of Steps Six and Seven until you are able to be more gentle with yourself.)

Spiritual Intimacy with God
(pages 67-69)

1. What is your definition of *prayer*?

2. Does your definition of *prayer* help or hinder your recovery? In what ways?

3. What is your definition of *meditation*?

4. Does your definition of *meditation* help or hinder your recovery? In what ways?

5. How can *prayer* and *meditation* be useful to you in recovery?

6. What does the phrase "*conscious contact with God*" mean to you?

7. Describe a time when you experienced this "*conscious contact with God:*"

8. How do you know when you have obtained *"knowledge of God's will"* for you?

9. Do you believe that it was *God's will* for you to find the Twelve Steps and to have a meaningful recovery?

Giving as Its Own Reward

(pages 71-76)

1. What is your definition of *a spiritual awakening*?

2. Does your definition of *a spiritual awakening* help or hinder your recovery? In what ways?

3. Have you experienced *a spiritual awakening*? If you have, describe your experience here:

4. If you have not experienced *a spiritual awakening*, what do you think is preventing you from having this kind of experience? What can you do to move beyond these barriers to spiritual growth?

5. What is your definition of *a spiritual experience?*

6. Does your definition of *a spiritual experience* help or hinder your recovery? In what ways?

7. Have you had what you would call *a spiritual experience*? If you have, describe your experience here:

8. What is your definition of *carrying the message*?

9. Does your definition of *carrying the message* help or hinder your recovery?

10. List twelve ways you have *carried the message* to others:

   (1)

   (2)

   (3)

   (4)

(5)

(6)

(7)

(8)

(9)

(10)

(11)

(12)

11. What areas of your life do you tend to keep separate from the Twelve Step Program? What are your reasons for doing this?

12. How can you *practice these principles* in all of your activities?

Other Recovery Topics

In addition to chapters on each of the Twelve Steps in *Hope and Recovery*, there are six related chapters in the text that are significant for anyone recovering from sex addiction or codependency to sex addiction. The questions that follow refer back to the *Hope and Recovery* text for three specific recovery topics: *Abstinence and Sobriety, Telling Others About Our Addiction*, and *The Slogans*.

(Note that *Hope and Recovery* text chapters on *Sponsorship*, *Slips/Relapses*, and *The Twelve Traditions* are not specifically referred to in this workbook. We do recommend, however, that you reread these three important chapters as preparation for the workbook questions that follow.)

Abstinence and Sobriety

(pages 77-82)

1. What is your definition of sexual *acting-out* or compulsive sex?

2. List behaviors that were a part of your active addiction and how they were harmful to you and/or others (in doing this, it will be helpful to reflect back to the First Step and Fifth Step):

3. What is your definition of *healthy sex*?

4. Which of the sexual behaviors you currently engage in are consistent with your definition of healthy sex? Which are not?

5. Are there some sexual behaviors that, early in your recovery, needed to be off-limits, but that you now can engage in without jeopardizing your recovery in any way? If so, what are these behaviors and why do you consider them healthy, allowable behaviors at this time?

6. Consider your life *one year* in the future: what is the role of healthy sexuality in your life at that future time?

7. Consider your life *five years* from now: what is the role of healthy sexuality in your life at that future time?

8. List some things you can do to improve the likelihood that healthy, joyful sexual activities will be an integral part of your life:

9. Choose a specific amount of time—a week, a month, or longer—and refrain from being genitally sexual during this period of time. Do not masturbate or engage in intercourse of any kind during this time. Prior to beginning this period of celibacy, record your thoughts, emotions, and expectations here:

10. Halfway through the period of time you have chosen for celibacy, record your thoughts, emotions, and expectations here. Indicate, also, what you expect the remaining time will be like:

11. What have you learned about yourself, your addiction, and your recovery so far during this period of celibacy?

12. At the end of the time period you chose to be celibate, record your thoughts and emotions here:

13. Through your experience, what have you learned about yourself, your addiction, and your recovery?

Telling Others about Our Addiction

(pages 93-98)

1. List here six people you are considering telling about your sex addiction:

   (1)

   (2)

   (3)

   (4)

   (5)

   (6)

2. Next, write down the possible benefit(s) of telling each person you have listed about your addiction:

3. Next, write down the possible harm that could come from telling each person you have listed about your addiction.(After discussing your list with another recovering person and noting his or her reaction to it, add or delete names from your list as appropriate.)

4. Next to the names of the people you've decided to tell about your addiction, indicate *how* you will tell each one:

5. After you actually tell these people of your sex addiction, record their reactions to you and, in turn, your response to their reactions.

The Slogans
(pages 99-108)

One Day at a Time

1. How often are you preoccupied with the past?

2. How often are you preoccupied with the future?

3. How can you make use of this slogan—*One Day at a Time*—in your daily life?

Easy Does It

1. How have you been "filled with despair, intolerance, rigidity, and impatience"?

2. How have you rationalized or otherwise justified procrastination?

Be Gentle with Yourself

1. How have you set extremely high expectations for yourself?

2. How can you adjust your expectations for yourself so that they will be more realistic?

3. How have you thought of yourself as a failure or worthless?

4. How have you punished yourself with negative self-talk and behaviors?

5. List some kind, gentle, nurturing things you can say to yourself *today*:

H.A.L.T.

1. How healthy are your eating habits? Do you continue to eat foods that affect you adversely?

2. Do you frequently eat too little or too much? How is your recovery affected when you are not properly nourished?

3. What role has anger played in your addiction?

4. What role has anger played in your recovery?

5. How can you improve your ability to express anger in a healthy and appropriate manner, then let it go?

6. What role has loneliness played in your addiction?

7. What role has loneliness played in your recovery?

8. What can you do to deal with and reduce the feelings of loneliness you experience?

9. How do you take care of your basic needs for adequate rest and sleep?

10. How do your relaxation habits affect your recovery?

First Things First

1. What are your priorities *today*?

2. How do sobriety and spiritual growth fit with your priorities?

Act As If

1. What aspects of recovery are particularly difficult for you at this time?

2. How can you make use of the *Act As If* slogan to cope with difficulties and challenges you face *today*?

If It Works, Don't Fix It

1. Read through the Twelve Steps (page 12 in the *Hope and Recovery* text.) List everything you think—or originally thought—was wrong with the Twelve Steps:

2. Discuss your objections to the Twelve Steps with your sponsor or another recovering person who has had a year or more of experience actively working the Steps. Ask how he or she has used the Twelve Steps, in spite of the shortcomings you've found in them. What have you learned about the Twelve Steps and yourself by doing this?

3. Read through the Twelve Traditions. List everything you think—or originally thought—is wrong with the Twelve Traditions:

4. Discuss your objections to the Twelve Traditions with your sponsor or another recovering person who has had a year or more of experience in the Program. Ask how he or she has used the Twelve Traditions, in spite of the shortcomings you have found in them. What have you learned about the Twelve Traditions and yourself by doing this?

This Too Shall Pass

1. How does time become distorted for you when you are acting out or are tempted to act out?

2. What aspects of your addiction or recovery have you thought were so hopeless and/or intolerable that you felt acting out would somehow help?

3. How can this slogan—*This Too Shall Pass*—help you cope during difficult times?

Let Go and Let God

1. What does *Let Go* mean to you?

2. How have you used the *Let Go and Let God* concept in your recovery?

3. List several things that you can let go of and let God handle *today*:

To Thine Own Self Be True

1. How authentic is your recovery?

2. In what ways have you been untrue to yourself in your recovery?

3. How can you make amends to yourself for not being true to yourself?

4. List several ways that you have been *true to yourself*:

Live and Let Live

1. List some examples of how you've sensed that you know how to run some else's life better than he or she knows how to run it:

2. How does this grandiosity fit with Steps Two and Three?

3. How does this grandiosity fit with Steps Six and Seven?

Keep It Simple

1. How have you tried to make recovery more complex than it is? What was the result?

2. List one or two—no more—ways that you can keep your recovery simple *today*:

There but for the Grace of God Go I

1. What is the difference between comparing yourself to another person and relating to another person?

2. How does this slogan—*There but for the Grace of God Go I*—help you heal? (In other words, how does it help you correct your grandiosity and your judgmental nature?)

Getting to Know Each Slogan

Pick one slogan that you find particularly interesting and write it down on seven separate pieces of paper. For the period of a week, carry one of the seven pieces of paper with you at all times. Place the other six pieces of paper in different locations where you will see them each day: on the bathroom mirror, on the refrigerator door, by your alarm clock, on your desk, on your dashboard, on the kitchen table.

Then, several times each day, take a few minutes to complete a ''spot inventory'' to see how you are using the slogan that day. When you pray, ask for knowledge of God's will for you in making the best use of this slogan. Each night, write how you have made use of this slogan during the day that has just passed.

Slogan No. 1:
(Ways I have made use of this slogan in my life this week)-

Day One:

Day Two:

Day Three:

Day Four:

Day Five:

Day Six:

Day Seven:

Now that you have used this particular slogan for a week's time, how is it affecting your recovery?

(After one week, choose a different slogan and repeat the process)

Slogan No. 2:
(Ways I have made use of this slogan in my life this week) -

Day One:

Day Two:

Day Three:

Day Four:

Day Five:

Day Six:

Day Seven:

Now that you have used this slogan for a week's time, how is it affecting your recovery?

Slogan No. 3:
(Ways I have made use of this slogan in my life this week) -

Day One:

Day Two:

Day Three:

Day Four:

Day Five:

Day Six:

Day Seven:

Now that you have used this particular slogan for a week's time, how is it affecting your recovery?

Slogan No. 4:
(Ways I have made use of this slogan in my life this week) -

Day One:

Day Two:

Day Three:

Day Four:

Day Five:

Day Six:

Day Seven:

Now that you have used this particular slogan for a week's time, how is it affecting your recovery?

Slogan No. 5:
(Ways I have made use of this slogan in my life this week) -

Day One:

Day Two:

Day Three:

Day Four:

Day Five:

Day Six:

Day Seven:

Now that you have used this particular slogan for a week's time, how is it affecting your recovery?

Slogan No. 6:
(Ways I have made use of this slogan in my life this week) -

Day One:

Day Two:

Day Three:

Day Four:

Day Five:

Day Six:

Day Seven:

Now that you have used this slogan for a week's time, how is it affecting your recovery?

Slogan No. 7:
(Ways I have made use of this slogan in my life this week) -

Day One:

Day Two:

Day Three:

Day Four:

Day Five:

Day Six:

Day Seven:

Now that you have used this slogan for a week's time, how is it affecting your recovery?

Slogan No. 8:
(Ways I have made use of this slogan in my life this week) -

Day One:

Day Two:

Day Three:

Day Four:

Day Five:

Day Six:

Day Seven:

Now that you have used this particular slogan for a week's time, how is it affecting your recovery?

Slogan No.9:
(Ways I have made use of this slogan in my life this week) -

Day One:

Day Two:

Day Three:

Day Four:

Day Five:

Day Six:

Day Seven

Now that you have used this particular slogan for a week's time, how is it affecting your recovery?

Slogan No. 10:
(Ways I have made use of this slogan in my life this week) -

Day One:

Day Two:

Day Three:

Day Four:

Day Five:

Day Six:

Day Seven:

Now that you have used this particular slogan for a week's time, how is it affecting your recovery?

Slogan No. 11:
(Ways I have made use of this slogan in my life this week) -

Day One:

Day Two:

Day Three:

Day Four:

Day Five:

Day Six:

Day Seven:

Now that you have used this particular slogan for a week's time, how is it affecting your recovery?

Slogan No. 12:
(Ways I have made use of this slogan in my life this week) -

Day One:

Day Two:

Day Three:

Day Four:

Day Five:

Day Six:

Day Seven:

Now that you have used this particular slogan for a week's time, how is it affecting your recovery?

Slogan No. 13:
(Ways I have made use of this slogan in my life this week) -

Day One:

Day Two:

Day Three:

Day Four:

Day Five:

Day Six:

Day Seven:

Now that you have used this particular slogan for a week's time, how is it affecting your recovery?

III. Personal Stories of Addiction, Hope and Recovery

The Twelfth Step encourages recovering people to carry the message to other sex addicts; the Preamble (adapted with permission of AA and printed on page 323 of the *Hope and Recovery* text) states that the Twelve Step fellowship is made up " . . . of women and men who share our experience, strength, and hope with each other that we may solve our common problem and help others recover from their sexual addictions."

Each of the personal stories written by recovering sex addicts for the *Hope and Recovery* text is unique, yet all eighteen stories share some basic similarities. As Frank points out in his story: " . . . the other sex addicts at the meeting were more *like* me than *unlike* me. The one thing we all had in common was the one thing that really mattered—we were sex addicts."

First-person recovery stories provide encouragement, as well as valuable information and insights. As you reread each story in the *Hope and Recovery* text and address the related questions in this workbook, focus on this consideration: *how the experiences of those who have gone before me can help me in my own continuing recovery*.

The eighteen sets of questions that follow were developed from the personal stories in *Hope and Recovery* written by recovering sex addicts.

Jim's Story
(pages 131-136)

1. Jim believes that his compulsive sexual behavior began very early in his life. At what time in your life did your sexual thoughts become obsessive and your sexual behaviors become compulsive?

2. As a consequence of his sexual acting-out behaviors, Jim eventually lost his job as a schoolteacher. How have your work performance and your career been affected by your sex addiction?

3. Jim recalls that in the early days of his Twelve Step group meetings for sex addicts, he and other men in his group were apprehensive about opening their meetings to female sex addicts. Do you have feelings of discomfort or fear about other recovering sex addicts attending your Twelve Step meetings? If so, what would you say these fears and feelings of discomfort relate to?

4. What can you do to overcome your feelings of discomfort or fear about other addicts and accept them into your fellowship?

5. It's one thing to work the Twelve Steps when life is unmanageable, another thing to continue working the Twelve Steps when a crisis has *passed* and life is going well. Jim refers to temporary respites from his addiction—times when he had virtually no urge to act out at all. Have you experienced respites from your addiction? How do you maintain commitment to your recovery program when things are going well in your life?

6. Jim has learned in recovery that for him, there is a difference between compulsive masturbation and healthy masturbation. In what ways have you learned to recognize the difference between compulsive sexual behaviors and healthy sexual behaviors in your own life?

7. What have you learned from Jim's story that will help you in your own recovery?

Ruth's Story
(pages 137-147)

1. Ruth believed that marriage and children would help to control—if not completely stop—her compulsive sexual behaviors. Prior to working the Twelve Steps, what did you believe would help to control or completely stop your own compulsive sexual behaviors?

2. Ruth used drugs in her efforts to control her sexual acting-out behaviors and she eventually became chemically dependent. Have you struggled with other compulsive or addictive behaviors in your efforts to control your own sexual acting-out behaviors?

3. Ruth's sexually compulsive behaviors and her chemical dependency interacted, making it extremely difficult for her to begin recovering from either addiction. If you struggle with other compulsive/addictive behaviors, are you working a recovery program to help you with these behaviors? Describe that program here:

4. Ruth learned that she could experience nonsexual intimacy with people in her Twelve Step fellowship. In recovery, what have you learned about nonsexual intimacy?

5. Ruth describes her fears of intimacy and sex. Do you have fears related to intimacy and sex? If so, describe these fears:

6. What have you learned from Ruth's story that will help you in your own recovery?

Joe's Story

(pages 149-154)

1. Joe tells of believing that sex was "dirty, sinful and wrong" and of being fearful of sex, all the while continuing to be driven and compulsive about sex. What negative attitudes have you had about sex? How have these negative attitudes about sex affected your recovery?

2. Joe cites a connection between his feelings of anger toward his mother and his sexual acting-out behaviors. How might your sex addiction be related to your own past experiences and relationships?

3. Joe describes what he learned in a treatment program for sex addicts. Have you ever sought professional help for your sex addiction? If so, what was your experience? How has this professional help affected your recovery?

4. What have you learned from Joe's story that will help you in your own recovery?

Rick's Story

(pages 155-163)

1. Rick tells about how he'd make rules to control his sexual behaviors, then modify or completely violate those rules almost immediately. How have you violated rules you've set for yourself relating to your sexual behaviors?

2. Rick's sexual fantasies changed from those of having a loving relationship with a woman, to those of exploitation and violence toward women. If your sexual fantasies changed over time, describe the nature of those changes here:

3. There was a pattern in Rick's behavior: he'd throw out his pornography collection, only to purchase new material again in a relatively short period of time. Have you used and/or collected pornography or other sexually explicit material? If so, how did your use and/or collection of this material relate to your addiction?

4. Rick has struggled with compulsive masturbation. What was the role of masturbation in your addiction? What is the role of masturbation in your recovery?

5. Rick explains how he erroneously *reversed* the Twelfth Tradition, placing personalities *before* principles in relation to his Twelve Step group. If you are a member of a Twelve Step group, how do you interact with people in the group who have been there for a longer period of time than you have been? How do you interact with people who are newcomers to the group?

6. Rick tells of consciously avoiding conflict in his Twelve Step group at one period of time in the group's evolution. How do you deal with conflict or potential conflict in your Twelve Step group?

7. What have you learned from Rick's story that will help you in your own recovery?

Jerome's Story
(pages 165-169)

1. Jerome recalls that when he was a child, his life looked very good to others, but was really very empty and lonely. Considering the significant gap that can exist between appearance and reality, how did your life look to others during your active addiction? And how did this appearance differ from the reality of your life at that time?

2. Jerome indicates that at first he had difficulty relating to other people in his Twelve Step group. How easily do you relate to others in your Twelve Step group? How do you see yourself as being different from other people in your group?

3. Jerome's acting-out behaviors involved equipment used in a ritualistic way. List any equipment and/or rituals for using it that your acting-out behaviors involved or required:

4. If you still have the equipment that you used in your acting-out behaviors, list here some reasons why you have kept this equipment and how doing so could be affecting your recovery:

5. If you have used equipment in your acting-out behaviors and *have* disposed of it, think back to the emotions you experienced when you did so and record them here:

6. What have you learned from Jerome's story that will help you in your own recovery?

Barbara's Story

(pages 171-179)

1. As a consequence of her sex addiction, Barbara almost lost her life. On several occasions she placed herself in dangerous situations and seriously considered suicide. In what ways have you put yourself at risk due to your compulsive sexual behaviors?

2. Barbara confused lust and sex addiction with love. Write something here about how you may have confused lust and addiction with love in your own life:

3. What do you believe is the difference between lust and love?

4. Barbara made use of the Fourth and Fifth Steps several times early in her recovery process. The first time she worked these steps, she focused on her anxiety, her grief, her shame, and the process of learning to accept support from other people in her group. How has anxiety been a part of your addiction? How has anxiety affected your recovery?

5. As you deal with your addiction in recovery, what losses do you find you need to grieve for? (e.g. places you went, activities you participated in, people you spent time with?)

6. How has shame been a part of your addiction? How does shame affect your recovery?

7. List some ways that you can get support from others while you are working on Steps Four and Five:

8. When Barbara had difficulty making use of the Eighth and Ninth Steps, she wisely returned to Steps Four and Five. In reworking the Fourth and Fifth Steps, she focused on her resentment, her self-righteousness, and her unwillingness to accept herself and others. Have these character defects been a part of your addiction? If so, in what ways?

9. What effect have your character defects had on your recovery?

10. What actions can you take to have these character defects removed?

11. The third time Barbara made use of the Fourth and Fifth Steps, she focused on improving her relationships with people outside the Twelve Step Program, with clergy, and with God. How comfortable are you with your relationships? What actions can you take to improve your relationships?

12. What have you learned from Barbara's story that will help you in your own recovery?

Charles's Story

(pages 181-191)

1. Charles recalls having had two standards for fidelity in his life: he expected his girlfriend to be faithful to him, but he believed it was acceptable for him to have sex with other women ''on the side''. Have you operated with double standards? If so, explain:

2. Charles attempted a ''geographic cure'' for his addiction by moving to another country. But he soon realized that he was a sex addict, regardless of where he lived. Have you ever attempted a ''geographic cure'' for your addiction? If so, explain:

3. Charles recalls always feeling let down and lonely after having sex with a prostitute. In reality, he wanted *more* than sex at these times. When you were acting out, what feelings did you experience after having sex with someone?

4. Consider the feelings you experienced after acting out sexually with someone—what does your reaction tell you about what you were seeking through your compulsive behavior?

5. In his postscript, Charles notes how different his life is since he began the recovery process. How is your life different now from the way it was prior to recovery?

6. Charles relates that he is proud of his standards and values. List the six values and standards that are most important to your life:

(1)

(2)

(3)

(4)

(5)

(6)

7. As you undertake a personal inventory, what do you think and feel about your values and standards? How will they help you in your recovery?

8. Charles tells of speaking with his children about his sex addiction and his recovery. How do you react to the way Charles handled this sensitive situation?

9. If you have children, what do they know about your acting-out behaviors? What do they know about your recovery?

10. What have you learned from Charles's story that will help you in your own recovery?

Allen's Story

(pages 193-201)

1. Allen tells of being "trapped" in relationships, unable to make healthy choices. How is this kind of repetitive cycle similar to your own past or current relationships?

2. Allen was arrested for exposing himself. Have you ever been arrested as a consequence of your sexual acting-out behaviors? If so, describe the most serious or shameful episode(s) here:

3. If you have not been arrested for your sexual acting-out behaviors, have you engaged in illegal sexual acts that you *could* have been arrested for? How were these illegal sexual acts related to your addiction?

4. Allen called himself names—names like ''worthless pervert.'' What disrespectful names have you called yourself? What negative self-talk have you engaged in?

5. What have you learned from Allen's story that will help you in your own recovery?

Jenny's Story
(pages 203-211)

1. Jenny tells of her isolation and of tolerating abusive relationships. Are the patterns and themes in your story similar in any way to hers? In what ways?

2. Jenny's compulsive sexual behavior involved self-abuse. Has your compulsiveness led to self-abuse?

3. Jenny led a double life—she acted one way when she was at work during the week, another way when she was home alone during weekends. Have you lived a double life because of your sex addiction? If so, how have you done this or attempted to do this?

4. Jenny was able to forgive the people who had hurt her. How forgiving are you of people who have hurt you? How is your forgiveness or reluctance to forgive affecting your recovery and your serenity?

5. In learning to accept herself, Jenny acknowledged her sexual orientation. Is your sexual orientation clear to you? What steps can you take to be more accepting of your sexual orientation and your sexuality in general?

6. What have you learned from Jenny's story that will help you in your own recovery?

Frank's Story

(pages 213-231)

1. Frank tells of having regrets about losing out on many experiences commonly associated with the teenage years. Do you believe that your compulsive sexual behavior negatively affected your ability to enjoy your childhood, your teenage years, and/or your early adulthood? If so, how do you feel about these issues now?

2. Time and time again, Frank told himself that he would stop being compulsive when some external condition was met—such as finding the right woman. How have you overlooked the seriousness of your addiction and sought out certain external conditions and circumstances on which to blame your compulsive behavior?

3. Frank's compulsive sexual behavior continued, even when he derived no pleasure or satisfaction from his sexual activities. If this has happened to you in relation to your addiction, describe your situation:

4. Frank was fearful that if he stopped acting out, he would lose his identity. How much a part of your identity or reputation are your compulsive sexual behaviors?

5. Frank kept a "stash" of pornography, "just in case". Do you have a stash of pornography or other cache of material or paraphernalia from your acting-out days, "just in case"? What does "just in case" mean for you?

6. Frank sexualized his emotions. Everything he *felt* was, in his mind, directly related to sex and the need to be sexual. Has this symptom of compulsivity evidenced itself in your life? In what ways?

7. Frank is careful not to "therapize"—in other words, he does not talk about therapy or theory from a professional point of view in his Twelve Step meetings. How often do you lose focus on the Twelve Steps in meetings? What can you do when you or others at Twelve Step meetings begin losing track of the Twelve Steps and the Program?

8. What have you learned from Frank's story that will help you in your own recovery?

Ryan's Story
(pages 233-238)

1. Ryan believes that his addiction was a "dominant force" in his life for nearly twenty years. How long have you struggled with obsessive sexual thoughts and addictive sexual behaviors?

2. Ryan used drugs to cope with his self-hatred and his addictive behaviors. Have you used alcohol and/or other drugs in attempts to cope with your emotions about yourself and your addictive behaviors?

3. Ryan rationalized his addictive behaviors by thinking of himself as "adventurous and sophisticated." How have you rationalized your own sexual acting-out behaviors?

4. Ryan was fearful that his double life would be discovered when he died. What possible discovery about yourself did you (or do you) fear most?

5. Ryan began to see that even his "victimless" acting-out behaviors were affecting him adversely. How have your "victimless" acting-out behaviors affected you?

6. In his story, Ryan shares the fact that he has had a slip and that he is not 100 percent in recovery. How do you respond to Ryan's ability to be gentle with himself and to focus on progress instead of perfection?

7. Ryan discovered that first he had to believe he was loved and okay, then he would stop acting out—not the other way around. What are your thoughts on this?

8. What have you learned from Ryan's story that will help you in your own recovery?

Jamie's Story

(pages 239-246)

1. Jamie's homosexuality led him, as a child, to regard himself as ''different'' from other boys. Is there anything about you that caused or causes you to think of yourself as different from others? How did your self-perception relate to your addiction? How did (or does) your self-perception affect your recovery?

2. Jamie worked very hard to protect his personal secrets. Have you maintained your own personal secrets? If so, how has this affected your addiction and your recovery?

3. Jamie considers himself gay, yet he had an ongoing sexual relationship with his wife. How do you explain a homosexual person having a sexual relationship with a person of the opposite sex?

4. What have you learned from Jamie's story that will help you in your own recovery?

Phil's Story

(pages 247-253)

1. Phil's acting-out behaviors involved pain and violence. Have pain and
    violence been themes in your addiction? If so, write about the role these
    themes have had in your thoughts and behaviors, then discuss them with
    another recovering addict. What does this tell you about yourself, your
    addiction, and your recovery?

2. Write about some gentle, nonaddictive images you have of safe, nurturing sex, then discuss them with another recovering addict. What does this tell you about yourself, your addiction, and your recovery?

3. Phil writes about how his addiction affected his relationship with his wife and his child. How has your compulsive sexual behavior affected important relationships in your life?

4. What have you learned from Phil's story that will help you in your own recovery?

Margret's Story

(pages 255-262)

1. Margret's story includes a series of accidents, school problems, institutionalizations, and a number of nameless sexual partners. Clearly, Margret was living in a self-destructive manner. The lives of many sex addicts are not as obviously out of control as Margret's life was. Is *your* story one of obvious desperation and repetitive destructive behaviors? Or did you lead a double life, such that the primary consequences of your addiction were *internal* in nature? Describe your situation here:

2. Margret's acting-out behaviors resulted in two unplanned and unwanted pregnancies. Have your addictive behaviors resulted in pregnancy? If so, what was the outcome of the pregnancy? What are your feelings *now* about this consequence of your addictive behavior?

3. What can you do as part of your Eighth and Ninth Step work to make amends to others and to forgive yourself as well?

4. Margret progressed from viewing sex as a ''powerful and uncontrollable weapon'' to viewing it as something based on ''sharing, giving and nurturing.'' How much progress are you making in learning to view sex as a healthy component of life, rather than as ''the enemy''?

5. Margret has turned her life of self-destruction and desperation into a life that is filled with pride, spirituality, gentleness, and love. How do you react as you read about the profound changes in Margret's life?

6. What have you learned from Margret's story that will help you in your own recovery?

Ken's Story

(pages 263-273)

1. Throughout his story, Ken tells of his loneliness prior to his addiction and during the period of his active addiction. What role has loneliness played in your life and your addiction?

2. How has being involved in a recovery program affected your feelings of loneliness?

3. Ken spent thousands of dollars on his addiction and eventually had major financial problems that affected his family. What effect did your addiction have on your attitudes about money? On your spending behavior? On your overall financial security?

4. Ken writes about a spiritual awakening he had as a result of his interaction with a clergyman he hadn't seen or talked to for years. What is your reaction to this story?

5. What have you learned from Ken's story that will help you in your own recovery?

Mark's Story
(pages 275-278)

1. Mark tells of being sexual with other men throughout his life, and all that time being heterosexual. Have you been sexual with people of your same sex, even though you are heterosexual? If so, how has this behavior affected your view of your own sexual orientation?

2. How do you explain a heterosexual person having sex with people of his/her own sex?

3. Several of the people who share their personal stories in *Hope and Recovery*—including Mark—note that they were physically or sexually abused as young children or teenagers. Did physical and/or sexual abuse in the earlier years of your life play a role in your addiction?

4. How do you think physical and sexual abuse relate to sex addiction?

5. What have you learned from studying Mark's story that will help you in your own recovery?

Liam's Story

(pages 279-289)

1. Liam refers to being a sex addict while he was still a virgin. What is your reaction to this?

2. What does Liam's story teach you about sex addiction?

3. Liam's girlfriend ended her relationship with him when he told her about his compulsive sexual behaviors. How have various people in your life reacted when they learned of your sex addiction?

4. Liam's addiction involved intense shame and repression related to sexual issues, including masturbation. In fact, part of Liam's recovery program was to learn how to masturbate. How do you react to this aspect of Liam's story?

5. What have you learned from Liam's story that will help you in your own recovery?

Alvin's Story
(pages 291-297)

1. Alvin was a minister, yet he was also living the life of a practicing sex addict. How do you react to this aspect of his story?

2. As a minister, Alvin used his position of authority and trust to initiate sexual relationships with members of his congregation—married and unmarried women and teenage girls. How do you react to this portion of his story?

3. Alvin attempted to "prove" that he wasn't a sex addict by focusing on what he *hadn't* done. Have you made conscious efforts to prove that you *don't* have a problem with your sexual behaviors? If so, how have you tried to do this?

4. What have you learned from Alvin's story that will help you in your own recovery?

The story that follows *(Jean's Story)* differs somewhat from the other eighteen personal stories in *Hope and Recovery*. Jean's compulsive behaviors were not so much about sex as they were about the following issues: compulsively searching for someone who would help her like herself and make her feel worthwhile; and desperately trying to control the sexual behaviors of another person. It is apparent in Jean's story, however, that her life became as unmanageable as a sex addict's life.

Many sex addicts have people very much like Jean in their lives—people who eventually become an integral part of the addictive denial and acting-out behaviors of the sex addict. Sex addicts and codependents have similar beliefs about sex, relationships, and self-worth. In fact, many sex addicts eliminate their compulsive sexual behaviors, then find that they have deeply entrenched codependent behavior patterns as well. In recovering from sex addiction, it is useful to understand codependency and to look at the part it may have played in the addiction itself, as well as how it may ''feed into'' a codependent person's behavior patterns.

For more information on codependency, check the Recommended Resources in this workbook. Note that the booklet *What Everyone Needs to Know about Sex Addiction* contains a series of lifestyle questions that characterize codependent behavior patterns.

Jean's Story
(pages 299-304)

1. Jean writes about her "pain, loneliness and acting out." How do you react to her story and to learning what it was like for her to be in a relationship with a sex addict?

2. Jean writes that she believed that sex was the only thing she had to offer people, that she was "loved" only when someone was sexual with her, and that her self-worth was based only on sex. Are Jean's beliefs similar in any way to your own? How are Jean's beliefs similar to those of the people you became involved with?

3. In her story, Jean describes her passive acting-out behaviors. Have you had partners who behaved in this way? If so, how did you respond to this behavior?

4. Jean believed that if she were only more attractive, more perfect, more sexually appealing, the person she was with would not continue to act out. In what ways have you reinforced these beliefs in the relationships you've had?

5. Early in recovery, Jean had ''some serious doubts'' about her relationship. If you are in a committed relationship with someone, how has *recovery* affected that relationship?

6. In what ways are your behaviors similar to Jean's? In what ways are your behaviors different from Jean's?

7. What have you learned from Jean's story that will help you in your own recovery?

A Message from the Author

In the first section of this workbook, you were asked to write a personal account of your acting-out history. Now that you have worked on the Twelve Steps and related recovery topics and have studied the stories of other recovering addicts, write your own story again—*without referring to your first version*.

In this second version of your story, focus on your *recovery* from sex addiction and how the Twelve Step Program has changed your life. Once you've completed this second version of your story, compare it with the first version you wrote. How has your perception of your addiction and your recovery changed?

Best wishes. You have now completed this workbook. Each question has required some work and reflection, as well as a careful, realistic look at addiction and recovery in your own life. May the joy and serenity of recovery continue to grow in you through all the days of your life.

—the author

Journal

This is the journal mentioned on page 42. Use it to record your nightly inventory for the period of one month. Try not to let concerns about grammar or style hinder the flow of your thoughts; the purpose of keeping a journal like this is simply to learn and grow.

Date:

Date:

Date:

Date:

Date:

Date:

Date:

Date:

Date:

Date:

Date:

Date:

Date:

Date:

Date:

Date:

Date:

Date:

Date:

Date:

Date:

Date:

Date:

Date:

Date:

Date:

Date:

Date:

Date:

Date:

Date:

Recommended Resources

The following resources provide additional information and help for sex addicts and codependents:

Anonymous. *Alcoholics Anonymous*. New York: A.A. World Services. 1976 (first printing, 1939).

Anonymous. *Twelve Steps and Twelve Traditions*. New York: A.A. World Services, 11th printing, 1972.

Carnes, Patrick. *Contrary to Love: Helping the Sexual Addict*. Minneapolis: CompCare Publishers, 1989.

Carnes, Patrick. *Out of the Shadows: Understanding Sexual Addiction*. Minneapolis: CompCare Publishers, 1983.

Fossum, M. and M. Mason. *Facing Shame: Families in Recovery*. New York: W.W. Norton & Company, 1986.

Grateful Members (Anonymous). The Twelve Steps for Everyone . . . who really wants them. Minneapolis: CompCare Publishers, 1977.

Halpern, Howard. *How to Break Your Addiction to a Person*. New York: Bantam, 1982.

Hunter, Mic. *Abused Boys: The Neglected Victims of Sexual Abuse*. Lexington, Massachusetts: Lexington Books, 1989.

Hunter, Mic, *The Twelve Steps and Shame*. Center City: Hazelden, 1988.

Hunter, Mic, *What Is Sex Addiction?* Center City: Hazelden, 1988.

Hunter, Mic and ''Jem''. *The First Step for People in Relationships with Sex Addicts*. Minneapolis: CompCare Publishers, 1989.

LeSourd, Sandra Simpson. *The Compulsive Woman*. New Jersey: Chosen Books, 1987.

Lloyd, Roseann and Richard Solly. *Journeynotes: Writing for Recovery and Spiritual Growth*. Center City: Hazelden, 1989.

Nelson, James. *Embodiment: An Approach to Sexuality and Christian Theology*. New York: The Pilgrim Press, 1978.

P.D.N.E.C. (Anonymous). *Hope and Recovery: A Twelve Step guide for healing from compulsive sexual behavior*. Minneapolis: CompCare Publishers, 1987.

P.D.N.E.C. (Anonymous). *What Everyone Needs to Know about Sex Addiction*. Minneapolis: CompCare Publishers, 1989.

Peele, Stanton. *Love and Addiction*. New York: New American Library, 1975.

Scannell, Mark. *The Intensive Journal: Taping the Creative Energy Within*. Minneapolis: Sycamore Publishing, 1983.